NARCISSISTIC

By Harvey Stuarts

NARCISSISTIC

Copyright © 2017 by Harvey Stuarts

All Rights Reserved. This document is geared towards providing exact and reliable information in regards to the topic and issue covered. The publication is sold with the idea that the publisher is not required to render accounting, officially permitted, or otherwise, qualified services. If advice is necessary, legal or professional, a practiced individual in the profession should be ordered.

- From a Declaration of Principles which was accepted and approved equally by a Committee of the American Bar Association and a Committee of Publishers and Associations.

In no way is it legal to reproduce, duplicate, or transmit any part of this document in either electronic means or in printed format. Recording of this publication is strictly prohibited and any storage of this document is not allowed unless with written permission from the publisher. All rights reserved.

The information provided herein is stated to be truthful and consistent, in that any liability, in terms of inattention or otherwise, by any usage or abuse of any policies, processes, or directions contained within is the solitary and utter responsibility of the recipient reader. Under no circumstances will any legal responsibility or blame be held against the publisher for any reparation, damages, or monetary loss due to the information herein, either directly or indirectly.

Respective authors own all copyrights not held by the publisher.

The information herein is offered for informational purposes solely, and is universal as so. The presentation of the information is without contract or any type of guarantee assurance.

The trademarks that are used are without any consent, and the publication of the trademark is without permission or backing by the trademark owner. All trademarks and brands within this book are for clarifying purposes only and are the owned by the owners themselves, not affiliated with this document.

Disclaimer and Terms of Use: The Author and Publisher has strived to be as accurate and complete as possible in the creation of this book, notwithstanding the fact that he does not warrant or represent at any time that the contents within are accurate due to the rapidly changing nature of the Internet. While all attempts have been made to verify information provided in this publication, the Author and Publisher assumes no responsibility for errors, omissions, or contrary interpretation of the subject matter herein.

Any perceived slights of specific persons, peoples, or organizations are unintentional. In practical advice books, like anything else in life, there are no guarantees of results. Readers are cautioned to rely on their own judgment about their individual circumstances and act accordingly.

This book is not intended for use as a source of legal, medical, business, accounting or financial advice. All readers are advised to seek services of competent professionals in the legal, medical, business, accounting, and finance fields.

TABLE OF CONTENTS

Introduction - Narcissistism 6

What Causes Narcissistic Personality Disorder? 8

How Do Children Become Narcissists? 11

The Narcissist and His Family 17

Narcissistic Relationships 22

How to Deal With a Narcissistic Partner 27

Understanding The Anatomy of a Personality 32

Confronting a Narcissist 34

In Love With Yourself: Dealing With Narcissistic Personalities at Work 37

The Narcissist's Ego Bruises Easily 40

Living in the Narcissist's Shadow 42

Separating From a Narcissistic Husband - One Effective Way to Empower Yourself 44

The Escalating Shamelessness of the Narcissist 46

Living With A Narcissistic Lawyer 48

10 Things You Should Know About Dealing With a Narcissist 50

Conclusion 54

INTRODUCTION: NARCISSISTM

Narcissism is the pursuit of gratification from vanity or egotistic admiration of one's own attributes. Narcissists focus on themselves primarily, set themselves above their partner, listen poorly, insist they are always right, and typically have poor skills for living as a life partner.

Narcissists, by definition, are folks who succumb to an it's all about me orientation to life. This orientation blocks ability to hear others. Somewhere along the line narcissists failed to grow out of the toddler's ego-centric assumption that what I want is all that matters.

Narcissists can be very generous. When it comes to disagreements however, my opinion, what I want, what I want you to do blocks absorption of information from others about their opinions and preferences. Thinking in either-or, winner-loser patterns worsens this problem. "I don't want to hear what you want or think because then I may not get my way or win the discussion."

To the extent especially that narcissistic people listens poorly to others, they may be difficult to live with as a life partner no matter how handsome, beautiful, and financially successful they may appear to be. The key antidote to narcissism is to train yourself to take others' perspectives seriously.

Retrain yourself to ask others what they think and feel. Seek to understand and become responsive to others' concerns when you and they differ.

As others answer your questions, focus on what makes sense about their perspective. Listen for what you can agree with. Comment favorably on what you can agree with before moving forward to add your own perspective.

To accomplish true listening you'll need to dump but from your vocabulary. But negates your prior agreement. It subtracts, dismisses and eliminates whatever came before, undoing your initial good efforts to understand others' points. Instead of using but, link others' thoughts and yours with either and or and at the same time. That way instead of indulging in the narcissistic patterns of ignoring and disputing others' viewpoints, you will begin to be able to add others' viewpoints to your own. I.e., you will begin to shift from narcissistic "My viewpoints are the only ones that count" to "There's two of us here and both of our perspectives matter."

Narcissism tends especially to block data regarding others' feelings. When a partner feels sad, anxious or upset, the narcissistic response is to personalize, that is, take the others' feelings as critical statements about themselves. If "it's all about me," what you feel must be about me as well. Narcissists therefore get mad instead of supportive when their partner expresses negative emotions like hurt or sad.

WHAT CAUSES NARCISSISTIC PERSONALITY DISORDER?

Narcissists are people who are extremely egocentric or self-centered. They are obsessed with their personal abilities and physical appearances. They have this strong belief that they are superior to other individuals.

Consequently, their self-esteem is easily threatened by negative feedbacks from other people. Narcissists hardly accept criticisms because they feel being overpowered by others. Likewise, they are close-minded about the idea of being defeated. When the previously mentioned behaviors become persistent and cause distress to a person's social life during adulthood, they become components of the condition called narcissistic personality disorder.

People with narcissistic personality disorder are indeed highly competent. Their self-confidence contributes enormously in every success they achieve in life. They are self- assured that they are versatile and capable of doing anything. They view themselves as extremely admirable and important beings. However, behind this self-confidence is a bunch of insecurity.

Narcissists feel humiliation and self-inadequacy when someone overshadows their abilities.

The cause of narcissistic personality disorder remains unknown. However, various researchers had determined contributory factors from childhood that might have lead to the development of this disorder.

1. OVERSENSITIVE PERSONA DURING CHILDHOOD

A person with narcissistic personality disorder exhibits an oversensitive character during childhood. This type of person easily becomes very emotional.

2. TOO MUCH PRAISE FOR PROFESSED OUTSTANDING APPEARANCE OR ABILITIES OF THE CHILD BY THE ADULTS

Adults have the tendency to over praise a child with outstanding appearance or looks. As a result, this child develops the feeling of superiority against others. Apart from this, the sense of supremacy triggers the child's manipulative and dominant behavior. However, commending the child's outstanding appearance or abilities has positive consequence as well, which is building up the child's self-confidence. On the other hand, excessive admiration can be a risk of making the child arrogantly confident. This is considered another factor that could possibly result to narcissistic personality disorder.

3. UNREALISTIC FEEDBACK ON BEHAVIORS

Adults may excessively honor positive conducts or excessively condemn negative conducts of a child. This makes the child oversensitive to criticisms. The fear of receiving negative comments encourages the child to continue the good behaviors. However, the child might consider any negative feedback as threat to his/her self-esteem.

4. BEING OVERVALUED BY PARENTS

In general, parents give great value to their child. In fact, the happiness and satisfaction of their child is usually their top priority. However, parents may become overprotective and overly generous sometimes. They have the habit of providing more than what their child desires. In the same way, they have the passion on making their child feel much secured. Consequently, being too much valued by parents may result to the child's selfish behavior. The child ends up considering himself/herself more excessively important than other people. This is also evident on individuals with narcissistic personality disorder.

The childhood behaviors that might be developed from the above mentioned factors could be considered normal depending on the child's age. However, such behaviors must be retained during childhood only. If they are still possessed by the person until adulthood and had severely affected the person's social life, then the person might have developed narcissistic personality disorder. There are no laboratory examinations to diagnose this disorder. On the other hand, mental health experts had developed a tool to categorize mental illness, including narcissistic personality disorder.

HOW DO CHILDREN BECOME NARCISSISTS?

I am often asked "What type of parenting leads children to grow up with a Narcissistic Personality Disorder?" Or "Are the children of Narcissistic parents at risk of becoming Narcissists themselves?" I thought that I would use today's post to shed some light on this issue.

HOW DOES SOMEONE "GET" A NARCISSISTIC PERSONALITY DISORDER?

Narcissistic Personality Disorders are a byproduct of certain childhood family environments. All children want their parents' approval and attention. Children adapt to their homes, and often the most productive and reasonable adaptation to some home situations is to become a Narcissist. Below are some common scenarios that can contribute to children becoming Narcissistic.

SCENARIO 1—NARCISSISTIC PARENTAL VALUES

In this situation the child is raised in a family that is very competitive and only rewards high achievement. One or both of the parents are Exhibitionist Narcissists. The family motto is: If you can't be the best, why bother?

Love is conditional: When you come in first in the race, win the science fair, or star in the school show, you are showered with praise and attention. When you do not, you are a disappointment. Everyone in the family is supposed to be special and prove it over and over again. No matter how much you achieve, the pressure is never off. As one woman said: "When I came home with a report card with all A's, my father asked me if anyone got an A+."

Children in these families do not feel stably loved. It is hard for them to enjoy anything for its own sake, if it does not confer status. Instead of being supported by their parents to explore what they like and want to do more of, they only receive support for high achievement. Their parents are not interested in their children's "real selves," they are mainly interested in how their children can make the family look good. They want to be able to brag to their neighbors: "Look at what my kid did!"

The children who grow up in homes like this only feel secure and worthwhile when they are successful and recognized as the "best." The conditional love of their childhood and the over evaluation of high status and success in their home sets in motion a lifelong pattern of chasing success and confusing it with happiness.

EXAMPLE: JOHN AND HIS RESUME LIFE

John, a brilliant and successful man with a Narcissistic Personality Disorder, told me that he was coming to therapy because he knew that had lost his way. Nothing he did seemed to have any real meaning for him. He said, "I have a resume life. Everything about me looks good on paper. Even my hobbies are cool. But somewhere along the way I lost touch with who I really am. I no longer feel much genuine pleasure in my accomplishments. I started out enjoying what I do well, but now I do it only because it impresses other people. Inside I feel empty."

SCENARIO 2: THE DEVALUING NARCISSISTIC PARENT

In this scenario there is a very domineering and devaluing parent who is always putting down the child. The parent is generally irritable, easily angered, and has unrealistically high expectations.

If there are two or more children, the parent will praise one and devalue the others. The "good one" can quickly become the "bad one" and suddenly a different sibling is elevated. Nobody in the family feels secure and everyone spends their time trying to pacify the explosive Narcissistic parent.

The other parent is often treated exactly like the children and belittled as well. When he or she disagrees with the Narcissistic parent, they too are devalued.

Children who grow up in these households feel angry, humiliated, and inadequate. They are likely to react to their childhood situation in a few different ways.

The Defeated Child: Some of these children simply give up and accept defeat. In their teenage years, after decades of being told that they are worthless, they may spiral down into a self-hating shame-based depression. Then to escape their inner shame, they may try to lose themselves in impulsive, addictive behaviors. Some become alcoholics and drug addicts, others spend their days on the internet. They never achieve their potential because they have been convinced that they have none.

The Rebellious Child: These children overtly reject their parents' message that they are "losers." Instead, they spend their life try to prove to themselves, the world, and the devaluing parent that they are special and their parents were wrong. They pursue achievement in every way that they can. Proving they are special becomes a lifelong mission, while underneath there is always a harsh inner voice criticizing their every mistake—no matter how minor.

The Angry Child: These children grow up furious at the devaluing parent. Anyone who reminds them of their parent in any way becomes the target of their anger. They sometimes become Toxic or Malignant Narcissists themselves. It is not enough for them to achieve, they must destroy as well.

EXAMPLE: THE MOVIE "PRETTY WOMAN"

In this movie the actor Richard Gere portrays a wealthy businessman who buys and breaks up companies. He enjoys destroying the life's work of the former owners of these companies because all of them are symbolic substitutes for his hated father. The movie turns into a Cinderella story after he hires a prostitute (played by Julia Roberts) with whom he eventually falls in love. Even his choice of a love object is typically Narcissistic. I have met many wealthy Narcissistic men who can only show love to women that they "save" who are safely below them in status.

SCENARIO 3: "THE GOLDEN CHILD"

These parents are usually closet Narcissists who are uncomfortable in the spotlight. Instead, they brag about their extremely talented child. Often the child is very talented and deserves praise, but these parents sometimes take it to ridiculous lengths. This type of excessive idealization of a child as flawless and special can lead to the child having a Narcissistic adaptation in later life.

THE EFFECTS OF CONDITIONAL VS. UNCONDITIONAL LOVE

Everyone wants to be seen realistically and loved unconditionally. If children believe that their parents only value them because they are special, this can contribute to an underlying insecurity. No one wins all the time. No one is better than everyone else in every way.

Children who are idealized by a parent can begin to believe that they are only lovable when they are perfect and worthy of idealization.

THE PERCEPTION OF FLAWS & SHAME

When parents idealize their children, the children may become ashamed when they see any flaws in themselves. This can lead them to keep striving for perfection and proof that they are flawless and worth idealizing.

STUNTED DEVELOPMENT OF THE REAL SELF

In this process, children may lose touch with their real selves and real likes and dislikes. Instead of exploring who they really are and where their true interests and talents lie, they can get off track entirely and spend their time only doing things that they are already good at and they think will get their parents' approval.

The Result: Too much parental idealization may lead to an unbalanced view of the self. When this happens, the child then perceives any flaws as unacceptable and strives to be seen as perfect. It is a short hop, skip, and a jump from this to full blown Narcissism

Occasionally, these children resist their role as "The Golden Child," do not become Narcissistic, and are embarrassed by the excessive praise that they receive. They feel burdened by the role that they are asked to play in the family. One mother told me: "My son is the flagship of the family who will lead us all to greatness." Her son told me: "I just want to get off this endless treadmill and live my own life without having to meet my parents' crazy expectations."

SCENARIO 4: THE EXHIBITIONIST'S ADMIRER

Some children grow up in a Narcissistic household where there is an Exhibitionist Narcissist parent who rewards them with praise and attention as long as they admire and stay subservient to the parent. These children are taught Narcissistic values, but are discouraged from exhibiting themselves for admiration. Instead their role in the family is to uncritically worship the greatness of their Narcissistic parent without ever trying to equal or surpass that parent's achievements.

This is an excellent way to create Covert or Closet Narcissists. The children learn that they will be given Narcissistic supplies—attention and praise—for not openly competing with the Narcissistic parent and that these supplies will be withheld and they will be devalued if they openly try to get acknowledged as special. All their value in the family comes from acting as a support to the ego of the Exhibitionist parent.

In adulthood, these children feel too exposed and vulnerable to be comfortable in the spotlight, so their Narcissism and self-esteem issues are less obvious to anyone who does not know them well. Some adapt to this role very well and lead productive lives in a job that involves supporting a high achieving Exhibitionist Narcissist whom they admire.

EXAMPLE: CINDI AND THE "GREAT MAN"

Cindi was the personal assistant of the CEO of her company. She admired him and lived to serve him. She felt special through association with him. She treasured any small bits of praise that she had received over the years from him and kept all the Holiday and Birthday cards that he had given her. Cindi never married because she was so focused on her job and had Narcissistic values herself. Whenever she met men who wanted to date her, they always seemed lacking compared to her boss. As she explained to one of her girlfriends, "After working so closely with my boss, other men just seem too inferior to bother with."

Punchline: Once you know what to look for, it is easy to see how certain childhood home environments support Narcissistic adaptations by the children. In some homes, becoming a Narcissist is often the only sane solution.

THE NARCISSIST AND HIS FAMILY

We are all members of a few families in our lifetime: the one that we are born to and the one(s) that we create. We all transfer hurts, attitudes, fears, hopes and desires - a whole emotional baggage - from the former to the latter. The narcissist is no exception.

The narcissist has a dichotomous view of humanity: humans are either Sources of Narcissistic Supply (and, then, idealised and over-valued) or do not fulfil this function (and, therefore, are valueless, devalued). The narcissist gets all the love that he needs from himself. From the outside he needs approval, affirmation, admiration, adoration, attention - in other words, externalised Ego boundary functions.

He does not require - nor does he seek - his parents' or his siblings' love, or to be loved by his children. He casts them as the audience in the theatre of his inflated grandiosity. He wishes to impress them, shock them, threaten them, infuse them with awe, inspire them, attract their attention, subjugate them, or manipulate them.

He emulates and simulates an entire range of emotions and employs every means to achieve these effects. He lies (narcissists are pathological liars - their very self is a false one). He acts the pitiful, or, its opposite, the resilient and reliable. He stuns and shines with outstanding intellectual, or physical capacities and achievements, or behaviour patterns appreciated by the members of the family. When confronted with (younger) siblings or with his own children, the narcissist is likely to go through three phases:

At first, he perceives his offspring or siblings as a threat to his Narcissistic Supply, such as the attention of his spouse, or mother, as the case may be. They intrude on his turf and invade the Pathological Narcissistic Space. The narcissist does his best to belittle them, hurt (even physically) and humiliate them and then, when these reactions prove ineffective or counter productive, he retreats into an imaginary world of omnipotence. A period of emotional absence and detachment ensues.

His aggression having failed to elicit Narcissistic Supply, the narcissist proceeds to indulge himself in daydreaming, delusions of grandeur, planning of future coups, nostalgia and hurt (the Lost Paradise Syndrome). The narcissist reacts this way to the birth of his children or to the introduction of new foci of attention to the family cell (even to a new pet!).

Whoever the narcissist perceives to be in competition for scarce Narcissistic Supply is relegated to the role of the enemy. Where the uninhibited expression of the aggression and hostility aroused by this predicament is illegitimate or impossible - the narcissist prefers to stay away. Rather than attack his offspring or siblings, he sometimes immediately disconnects, detaches himself emotionally, becomes cold and uninterested, or directs transformed anger at his mate or at his parents (the more "legitimate" targets).

Other narcissists see the opportunity in the "mishap". They seek to manipulate their parents (or their mate) by "taking over" the newcomer. Such narcissists monopolise their siblings or their newborn children. This way, indirectly, they benefit from the attention directed at the infants. The sibling or offspring become vicarious sources of Narcissistic Supply and proxies for the narcissist.

An example: by being closely identified with his offspring, a narcissistic father secures the grateful admiration of the mother ("What an outstanding father/brother he is"). He also assumes part of or all the credit for baby's/sibling's achievements. This is a process of annexation and assimilation of the other, a strategy that the narcissist makes use of in most of his relationships.

As siblings or progeny grow older, the narcissist begins to see their potential to be edifying, reliable and satisfactory Sources of Narcissistic Supply. His attitude, then, is completely transformed. The former threats have now become promising potentials. He cultivates those whom he trusts to be the most rewarding. He encourages them to idolise him, to adore him, to be awed by him, to admire his deeds and capabilities, to learn to blindly trust and obey him, in short to surrender to his charisma and to become submerged in his follies-de-grandeur.

It is at this stage that the risk of child abuse - up to and including outright incest - is heightened. The narcissist is auto-erotic. He is the preferred object of his own sexual attraction. His siblings and his children share his genetic material. Molesting or having intercourse with them is as close as the narcissist gets to having sex with himself.

Moreover, the narcissist perceives sex in terms of annexation. The partner is "assimilated" and becomes an extension of the narcissist, a fully controlled and manipulated object.

Sex, to the narcissist, is the ultimate act of depersonalization and objectification of the other. He actually masturbates with other people's bodies.

Minors pose little danger of criticizing the narcissist or confronting him. They are perfect, malleable and abundant sources of Narcissistic Supply. The narcissist derives gratification from having coital relations with adulating, physically and mentally inferior, inexperienced and dependent "bodies".

These roles - allocated to them explicitly and demandingly or implicitly and perniciously by the narcissist - are best fulfilled by ones whose mind is not yet fully formed and independent. The older the siblings or offspring, the more they become critical, even judgemental, of the narcissist. They are better able to put into context and perspective his actions, to question his motives, to anticipate his moves.

As they mature, they often refuse to continue to play the mindless pawns in his chess game. They hold grudges against him for what he has done to them in the past, when they were less capable of resistance. They can gauge his true stature, talents and achievements - which, usually, lag far behind the claims that he makes.

This brings the narcissist a full cycle back to the first phase. Again, he perceives his siblings or sons/daughters as threats. He quickly becomes disillusioned and devaluing. He loses all interest, becomes emotionally remote, absent and cold, rejects any effort to communicate with him, citing life pressures and the preciousness and scarceness of his time.

He feels burdened, cornered, besieged, suffocated, and claustrophobic. He wants to get away, to abandon his commitments to people who have become totally useless (or even damaging) to him. He does not understand why he has to support them, or to suffer their company and he believes himself to have been deliberately and ruthlessly trapped.

He rebels either passively-aggressively (by refusing to act or by intentionally sabotaging the relationships) or actively (by being overly critical, aggressive, unpleasant, verbally and psychologically abusive and so on). Slowly - to justify his acts to himself - he gets immersed in conspiracy theories with clear paranoid hues.

To his mind, the members of the family conspire against him, seek to belittle or humiliate or subordinate him, do not understand him, or stymie his growth. The narcissist usually finally gets what he wants and the family that he has created disintegrates to his great sorrow (due to the loss of the Narcissistic Space) - but also to his great relief and surprise (how could they have let go someone as unique as he?).

This is the cycle: the narcissist feels threatened by arrival of new family members - he tries to assimilate or annex of siblings or offspring - he obtains Narcissistic Supply from them - he overvalues and idealizes these newfound sources - as sources grow older and independent, they adopt anti narcissistic behaviours - the narcissist devalues them - the narcissist feels stifled and trapped - the narcissist becomes paranoid - the narcissist rebels and the family disintegrates.

This cycle characterises not only the family life of the narcissist. It is to be found in other realms of his life (his career, for instance). At work, the narcissist, initially, feels threatened (no one knows him, he is a nobody). Then, he develops a circle of admirers, cronies and friends which he "nurtures and cultivates" in order to obtain Narcissistic Supply from them. He overvalues them (to him, they are the brightest, the most loyal, with the biggest chances to climb the corporate ladder and other superlatives).

But following some anti-narcissistic behaviours on their part (a critical remark, a disagreement, a refusal, however polite) - the narcissist devalues all these previously idealized individuals. Now that they have dared oppose him - they are judged by him to be stupid, cowardly, lacking in ambition, skills and talents, common (the worst expletive in the narcissist's vocabulary), with an unspectacular career ahead of them.

The narcissist feels that he is misallocating his scarce and invaluable resources (for instance, his time). He feels besieged and suffocated. He rebels and erupts in a serious of self-defeating and self-destructive behaviours, which lead to the disintegration of his life.

Doomed to build and ruin, attach and detach, appreciate and depreciate, the narcissist is predictable in his "death wish". What sets him apart from other suicidal types is that his wish is granted to him in small, tormenting doses throughout his anguished life.

NARCISSISTIC RELATIONSHIPS

Since writing "Codependency for Dummies, countless people contact me about their unhappiness and difficulties in dealing with a difficult loved one, frequently a narcissistic partner or parent who is uncooperative, selfish, cold, and often abusive. Partners of narcissists feel torn between their love and their pain, between staying and leaving, but they can't seem to do either. They feel ignored, uncared about, and unimportant. As the narcissist's criticism, demands, and emotional unavailability increase, their confidence and self-esteem decrease. Despite their pleas and efforts, the narcissist appears to lack consideration for their feelings and needs. Over time, they become deeply hurt and frustrated. When the narcissist is a parent, by the time their children reach adulthood, the emotional abandonment, control, and criticism that they experienced growing up has negatively affected their self-esteem and capacity for achieving success or sustaining loving, intimate relationships.

The term narcissism is commonly used to describe personality traits among the general population, usually someone who is selfish or seeks attention. Actually, a degree of healthy narcissism makes a well-balanced, strong personality. On the other hand, a narcissistic personality disorder (NPD) is much different and requires specific criteria that must be met for a diagnosis. It only affects a small percentage of people - more men than women. As described in "Do You Love a Narcissist?" Someone with NPD is grandiose (sometimes only in fantasy), lacks empathy, and needs admiration from others, as indicated by five of these summarized characteristics:

A grandiose sense of self-importance and exaggerates achievements and talents

1. Dreams of unlimited power, success, brilliance, beauty, or ideal love
2. Lacks empathy for the feelings and needs of others
3. Requires excessive admiration
4. Believes he or she is special and unique, and can only be understood by, or should associate with other special or of high-status people (or institutions)
5. Unreasonably expects special, favorable treatment or compliance with his or her wishes
6. Exploits and takes advantage of others to achieve personal ends
7. Envies others or believes they're envious of him or her
8. Has "an attitude" of arrogance or acts that way

The disorder also varies from mild to extreme. But of all the narcissists, beware of malignant narcissists, who are the most pernicious, hostile, and destructive. They take traits 6 & 7 to an extreme and are vindictive and malicious. Avoid them before they destroy you.

CHILDREN OF NARCISSISTS

Narcissistic parents usually run the household and can do severe damage to the self-esteem and motivation of their children. Often they attempt to live vicariously through them. These parents expect excellence and/or obedience, and can be competitive, envious, critical, domineering, or needy. Although their personalities differ, the common factor is that their feelings and needs, particularly emotional needs, come first. As a result, their children learn to adapt, become codependent. They bear the responsibility for meeting the parent's emotional needs, rather than vice versa.

Whereas their parents feel entitled, they feel unentitled and self-sacrifice and deny their own feelings and needs (unless they, too, are narcissistic). They don't learn to trust and value themselves and grow up alienated from their true selves. They may be driven to prove themselves in order to win their parents' approval, but find little motivation to pursue their wants and goals when not externally imposed (e.g., by a partner, employer, teacher).

Although they may be unaware of what was missing in their childhood, fear of abandonment and intimacy continues to permeate their adult relationships. They're afraid of making waves or mistakes and being authentic. Used to seeking external validation, many become pleasers, pretending to feel what they don't and hiding what they do. By reenacting their family drama, they believe their only choice is to be alone or give up themselves in a relationship.

Often adult children of narcissistic parents are depressed, have unacknowledged anger, and feelings of emptiness. They may attract an addict, a narcissist, or other unavailable partner, repeating the pattern of emotional abandonment from childhood. Healing requires recovery from codependency and overcoming the toxic shame acquired growing up in a narcissistic home.

PARTNERS OF NARCISSISTS

Partners of narcissists feel betrayed that the considerate, attentive and romantic person they fell in love with disappeared as time went on. They feel unseen and lonely, and long for emotional connection. In varying degrees, they find it difficult to express their rights, needs, and feelings and to set boundaries. The relationship reflects the emotional abandonment and lack of entitlement they experienced in childhood. Because their boundaries weren't respected growing up, they're highly sensitive to criticism and defenseless to narcissistic abuse. As their relationship progresses, partners admit feeling less sure of themselves than they once did. Uniformly, their self-esteem and independence steadily decline. Some give up their studies, career, hobbies, family ties, or friends to appease their partner.

Occasionally, they experience remembrances of the warmth and caring from the person with whom they first fell in love-often brilliant, creative, talented, successful, handsome or beautiful. They don't hesitate to say that they're committed to staying in the relationship, if only they felt more loved and appreciated. For some people, divorce is not an option. They may be co-parenting with an ex, staying with a spouse for parenting or financial reasons, or they want to maintain family ties with a narcissistic or difficult relative. Some want to leave, but lack the courage.

NARCISSISTIC ABUSE

Narcissists use defenses to hide their deep and usually unconscious shame. Like bullies, They protect themselves through aggression and by wielding power over others.

Malignant narcissists are maliciously hostile and inflict pain without remorse, but most narcissists don't even realize they've injured those closest to them, because they lack empathy. They're more concerned with averting perceived threats and getting their needs met. Consequently, they aren't aware of the hurtful impact of their words and actions.

For example, one man unbelievably couldn't understand why his wife, whom he had long cheated on, wasn't happy for him that he had found joy with his paramour. It was only when I pointed out that most women wouldn't be pleased to hear that their spouse was enjoying sex and companionship with another woman that he suddenly grasped the error of his thinking. He had been blinded by the fact that he'd unconsciously sought his wife's blessings, because his narcissistic mother never approved of his girlfriends or choices.

Narcissistic abuse can include any type of abuse, whether physical, sexual, financial, mental, or emotional abuse. Most often it involves some form of emotional abandonment, manipulation, withholding, or other uncaring behavior. Abuse can range from the silent treatment to rage, and typically includes verbal abuse, such as blaming, criticizing, attacking, ordering, lying, and belittling. It may also include emotional blackmail or passive-aggressive behavior. If you're experiencing domestic or intimate partner violence, read "The Truth about Domestic Violence and Abusive Relationships," and seek help immediately.

TREATMENT

Not many narcissists enter therapy unless they're pressured by a partner or suffer an extreme blow to their image or self-esteem. As described in my peer-reviewed article, treating a narcissist requires considerable skill.

However, even if the narcissist refuses to get help or change, your relationship can markedly improve by changing your perspective and behavior. In fact, learning about NPD, raising your self-esteem, and learning to set boundaries are just a few of the many things you can do to significantly better your relationship.

HOW TO DEAL WITH A NARCISSISTIC PARTNER

Some narcissists are obviously obnoxious, offensive and obstinate. Others, however, present as attractive, appealing, easy-going people. It's not until a direct confrontation occurs that their narcissism becomes obvious.

Summon up the courage to tell him (or her) that he's being self-centered and he'll either continue doing whatever he was doing as if you hadn't said anything at all or he will become irate. "Me? Me? Self-centered? How do you think that makes ME feel?"

Though all narcissists are not cut from the same cloth, they do have many traits in common. Here are the most typical ones:

1. Narcissists find it hard (if not impossible) to truly appreciate the validity of another's point of view. They imagine that others think and feel the same way they do. And if they don't, something's wrong with them.

2. Narcissists need constant validation from the outside. Admire and respect them and they do fine. Find fault with them and watch out! Grandiose narcissists will strike back venomously; closet narcissists will shrink back into their cave.

3. Narcissists often display a façade self based on impressive and admirable traits. What's wrong with that? Nothing, if it weren't mere window dressing. Their façade self is fake, covering up a real self that's insecure and vulnerable.

4. Narcissists view others as extensions of themselves. The narcissist sets the standards of behavior and does not tolerate opposition - especially if your viewpoint requires him to respond in ways he doesn't wish to.

5. Narcissists believe that they are entitled to special treatment. Whether it's a "stupid" law, or a "dumb" demand, narcissists feel that they shouldn't have to go along with the pack and conform. They believe they are of higher status; therefore why adapt just to please someone else.

6. Narcissists use money to help them feel special. Status items such as expensive clothes, cars, homes, dinners and trips are essential ways that a narcissist enhances his ego. Spending money, if you have it, is one thing; spending money, if you don't have it, is another. Regardless, a narcissist believes that he deserves the best. And easily fools himself into believing that the money will be there in the future, even if it's not there right now.

7. Narcissists may make a show of being generous by being big tippers or taking care of bills. Look closely, however, and you'll see that their generosity is based upon establishing a reputation for themselves as a VIP.

It may seem weird to say "discover" that you're living with a narcissist, but it's true. Many people don't realize that their partner (or parent or adult child) is a narcissist, discovering it only after much time has elapsed. Why isn't it obvious at the very beginning?

TWO REASONS:

1. Narcissists are great masters of disguise, describing their behavior in the best of terms, (i.e. I'm only doing it for you!) Hence, it may take awhile for you to 'get' what's really going on.

2. Though narcissism has a bad rep (egocentric, egotistical), narcissists also have positive traits. Indeed, they may be quite charismatic and charming. Hence, it may be hard to believe that narcissism is driving their behavior.

Once you recognize that you are living with a narcissist, here are 7 valuable tips for you to maintain your sanity and self-esteem.

1. KNOW WHAT YOU WILL TOLERATE AND WHAT YOU WON'T

Trust your own judgment. If he (or she) is spending recklessly, know what you will tolerate and what you won't. That doesn't mean that all spending has to be done your way (unless you're 2 narcissists battling it out). But it does mean that you don't tolerate the narcissist's explanation for free-spending (i.e. Hey, you only live once.") And you take necessary steps (whether he likes it or not)to protect your financial future.

2. BOLSTER YOUR OWN SELF-ESTEEM

Do not expect your narcissist to build up your self-esteem when he has just helped tear it down. That is something you must do for yourself. Spend more time with people who think well of you. Get involved with pleasurable activities that bolster your ego. Be kind to yourself.

3. KNOW WHEN YOU'RE BEING 'GASLIGHTED'.

When your narcissist says something, then later denies saying it or claims to have said something different, you can begin to doubt your own sanity. Were you listening? Were you dreaming? Is she nuts? Am I nuts? What's going on here? Your narcissist may be doing this maliciously to throw you off balance. Or, she may simply be responding to her need of the moment, forgetting what she previously said.

4. DEVELOP A POSITIVE SUPPORT SYSTEM

It may be hard to be honest with others. You may feel embarrassed, especially if you've been covering for your narcissist for so long. Nevertheless, see if there's a trustworthy friend or family member with whom you can share what's really going on. Also, consider seeking the help of a professional who will be able to offer you objective feedback.

5. DON'T TOLERATE DENIGRATING EMOTIONAL OUTBURSTS

At times you will be upset with each other and need to let off steam. But "how" one lets off steam is vital. If you're being spoken to with disdain and disrespect, stop the action. Make the issue, HOW you are being treated. Express your disappointment. Demand an apology. And if necessary, walk away, letting it be known that you'll be happy to pick up where you left off when you're treated with respect.

6. LEARN THE SKILLS OF NEGOTIATION

Just because your narcissist wants something, doesn't mean she needs to get it. Just because she expresses herself forcefully, doesn't mean you fold. Everything is negotiable.

You just need to know where your power lies. Then you need to convey it and enforce it. The skills of negotiation will empower you in many areas of life - today and in your future.

7. ACCEPT THAT YOU ARE NOT GOING TO DO A TOTAL MAKEOVER OF YOUR NARCISSIST'S PERSONALITY.

Nor should you want to. If your relationship is that bad, consider splitting. But, if there are redeeming traits, see if you can work together to create "family rules" of acceptable behavior.

Living with a narcissist is not easy. But putting into practice these 7 rules will make things more manageable for you.

UNDERSTANDING THE ANATOMY OF A PERSONALITY

In the Enneagram system of personality, one of the 9 types is our main one. We also have a special connection to four other types: our two wings and two arrows. Since I'm a 5-Observer, my wings are type 4-Romantic and type 6-Questioner. My arrows are type 7-Adventurer and type 8-Asserter.

Every now and then I rate the order of strengths of all 9 types in my own personality:

5 - I've always been quiet, curious, introverted, and shy. I'm an INFP (introverted, intuitive, feeling, perceiving) with almost as strong Thinking as Feeling. My father, an INTJ scientist, a 5 with a strong 6 wing, had a big influence on me. His Feeling function was developed in some ways – he was idealistic and a humanitarian – but weak in others - he didn't like to read novels or watch plays, and had no tolerance for strong displays of feeling. My life is more influenced by my 4-Romantic wing – I love the arts and psychology.

4 – My second type in importance is my 4-wing, the Romantic, especially when it comes to the artistic and compassionate sides of life. I was drawn to the piano early, majored in music at the University, and taught piano for many years. I almost never get depressed, however, and I'm not a dramatic kind of person.

9 – I relate to how type 9-Peace Seekers often appreciate nature and embody spirituality. I also relate to the 9's distaste for conflict. And I have trouble making up my mind.

My mother was probably a 9 or a 2.

1 - I'm idealistic as 1-Perfectionists are, but not a reformer. Like Ones, I can be meticulous about some things. My father was critical of my school-work and tried to teach me to be logical and exacting. My mother tried to teach me to be a neat housekeeper (her One-wing) and only partially succeeded.

6 – I'm not very paranoid but I am sometimes fearful, cautious, and uncertain. I also relate to the anti-authoritarian attitude of some 6's.

7 – When I feel like a 7-Adventurer all my cares fly away and life is great. I love feeling uninhibited and being in the moment, especially when I'm playing the piano, drawing, or hanging out with friends. This is one of my arrows.

2 - Like many females my age, I was pressured somewhat to act like a Helper but my life isn't organized around helping others. I'm not as diplomatic or sociable as most 2's I've known.

8 – Going toward my 8-Asserter arrow is growthful for me, but you would never mistake me for an 8. One reason I fell in love with the Enneagram was that I already knew I needed to become more confident, assertive, and outspoken, like many 8's are.

3 I'm least of all like the 3-Achiever. Ambition, materialism, obsession with success, and marketing myself scare me. Being intrigued and happy with what I'm doing is much more appealing to me than success or making a splash. I'm still trying to understand the 3 part of me.

CONFRONTING A NARCISSIST

A narcissist has two faces, the abuser behind closed doors and the lovely person every one else knows. This is a very clever way to protect themselves if the abused ever speaks out. Generally you will find that no one believes the abused, narcissist's always puts the abused on a pedestal to others, It makes it very difficult when the abused finally tries to speak out.

A Narcissist will never admit they have a problem, if confronted with their own bad behaviour they will do their very best to make people believe they are the victim.

If they are backed into a corner with the unavoidable truth about their bad behaviour they will begin to manipulate people by sulking and crying, this is designed to distract people from the truth and make people see the narcissist as an upset mess.

When you are confronted by someone who is crying and upset it is human nature to try and comfort them, this is playing right into their hands.

They will say things like "How can they be doing this to me", "I don't deserve this", "I can't believe this is happening to me, why are they doing this to me?"

The narcissist knows full well why it is happening, but as their life is nothing but lies, the person who they are talking to usually does not.

Before you know it, YOU are the bad person for making them feel so bad, the reason it all started is forgotten about, the tables have turned and now you are the one who is expected to apologise.

This behaviour can go on for days, weeks, months or years. As long as it takes for them to get the result they need.

Once a narcissist no longer has any use for you or feels you can no longer offer their narcissistic supply they will begin their smear campaign.

Whatever narcissist's perceive to be your psychological or situational "weak spots" will be their prime targets. Whether it be your family, friends or work colleagues they will do their best to paint you in a bad light.

As a last resort the narcissist becomes pathetic.

When they are confronted with unavoidable consequences for their own bad behavior, including your anger, they will melt into a soggy puddle of weepy helplessness.

It's all their fault. They can't do anything right. They feels so bad. What they don't do: own the responsibility for their bad conduct and make it right. Instead, as always, it's all about them, and their helpless self-pitying weepiness, dumping the responsibility for her consequences AND for their unhappiness about it on you.

As so often with narcissist's, it is also a manipulative behavior. If you fail to excuse their bad behavior and make them feel better, YOU are the bad person for being cold, heartless and unfeeling when they feel so awful.

Once you have discovered that the person in your life is a narcissistic and you feel that you can no longer take the abuse, there are two options.

LOW CONTACT OR NO CONTACT

Please note that most people who choose Low Contact usually end up No Contact very soon after.

If you are going to go Low Contact or No Contact firstly make sure you are safe, if you feel you are in danger at any point get out of the situation and if you need to, call the police.

Confide in a close friend first, tell them about your situation and explain to them what you plan to do. Make sure the friend is not friends with the narcissist as they might just tell them what you are planning to do.

IN LOVE WITH YOURSELF: DEALING WITH NARCISSISTIC PERSONALITIES AT WORK

Love is an interesting business subject. I've written about loving your job, being in love with a co-worker or working with a spouse you love. But what if you are working with someone who is totally self-involved, in love with him or herself... a narcissist?

We may toss the term around, but narcissism is a real psychological condition in which one has an excessive interest in oneself-far beyond what is normal. While positive self-esteem is important, there's a big difference between having a positive self-image and believing in one's superiority to others.

The term comes from a Greek myth about the beautiful Narcissus. Upon seeing his own reflection in a pool he fell in love with it. He didn't know it was his own image and fell in the water and drowned because he was unable to stop looking at himself.

A narcissist, while often entertaining, puts strain on relationships. It becomes especially difficult in a professional environment where people's financial futures are on the line.

Having a boss or co-worker who feels that he or she is the "smartest" or "most accomplished," can manifest itself in a refusal to listen to other's ideas or a need for constant praise. This person can be overly sensitive to clients' criticism and that not only makes for bad personal relationships, it makes for bad business.

Wondering if you're working with (or are) a real, clinical narcissist? Here's a fun test from the Diagnostic and Statistical Manual of Mental Disorders (DSM) to determine narcissistic personality disorder. A clinical narcissist, according to the manual, has five or more of the following traits I summarize here:

1. Has a grandiose sense of self-importance (e.g., exaggerates achievements and talents, expects to be recognized as superior without commensurate achievements).

2. Is preoccupied with fantasies of unlimited success, power, brilliance, beauty or ideal love.

3. Believes that he or she is "special" and unique and can only be understood by, or should associate with, other special or high status people (or institutions).

4. Requires excessive admiration.

5. Has a sense of entitlement, i.e., unreasonable expectations of especially favorable treatment or automatic compliance with his or her expectations.

6. Is interpersonally exploitative, i.e., takes advantage of others to achieve his or her own ends.

7. Lacks empathy: is unwilling to recognize or identify with the feelings and needs of others.

8. Is often envious of others or believes that others are envious of him or her.

9. Shows arrogant, haughty behaviors or attitudes.

Seriously, it's very unlikely that your co-worker or boss is a clinical or Gordon Gekko-style narcissist. Most normal people are likely to have at least a few of these traits and even those can be annoying. At this point you may be asking yourself: what's the next logical step to overcome the power of narcissism? There are a few ways to manage a relationship with a narcissistic person in your life.

Primarily, recognize that extreme narcissists are not interested in you and it's not about you. Accept their emotional limitations. As soon as you accept that, your relationship will be easier. Don't take things too personally. They probably aren't thinking about you, your feelings or your reaction.

Communicate with care. Negativity is difficult for the narcissist.

Understand their motivations. Is it money, power, relationships or physical attractiveness? When you understand what drives the self-absorption, you can learn to work with it.

Know you probably can't outmaneuver, out-charm or out-work a narcissist. They are most likely very motivated and socially skilled.

You cannot please a narcissist. They are by nature unsatisfied.

If you are in a work situation, you might just have to accept someone with a narcissistic personality for who they are. As long as you take care not to expect too much emotionally, you might just be able to sit back and tolerate their ramblings about me, myself and I.

THE NARCISSIST'S EGO BRUISES EASILY

We all have egos. The ego is the psychological "I" within us, an integral part of our identity. Strong egos are important. They tell us that we are valuable, competent, and solid inside. The ego is formed from early childhood. It develops as a result of positive, consistent, loving interactions with the parent(s). If a child feels wanted and is treated with love and respect, he feels positive and secure about himself. He values his uniqueness as a reflection of his parents' communication of this to him through their consistent words and behaviors.

Some children have damaged egos. They feel diminished, insecure, and ashamed. They have great difficulty asserting themselves. They stay in the background, unable to speak up for themselves or defend themselves when they have been wronged. Inside they feel fragile, small and insignificant.

The narcissist has a highly inflated ego. He experiences himself as vastly superior, more intelligent, talented, creative, and attractive than others. The narcissist's sense of self importance has no limits. He is unaware and unconcerned about the feelings of others. All that matters is that he gets what he wants.

His sense of self is grandiose to the point of being delusional. He engages in endless self talk: a running torrent of his brilliant ideas and accomplishments.

"The narcissist expects others to mirror him perfectly...he expects you, in your words, gestures, and actions, to feed back to him his flawless vision of himself." If the narcissist thinks that you have failed to acknowledge his perfection and superiority, he feels emotionally bruised and injured. Even the smallest oversight on the part of a business partner, family member, spouse or friend is felt by the narcissist as a wound. The narcissist has been slighted. Inside he feels diminished. As a result, he is enraged. Although the narcissistic ego is grandiose, it is brittle. It lacks elasticity and flexibility.

Those who have a healthy pliable ego can tolerate the slings and arrows that strike us all the time. Humor is the soothing balm, the respite, the exquisite poke that allows us to laugh at ourselves. The narcissist may appear to make fun of himself but this is disingenuous. He is not capable of experiencing the joy of a fully developed sense of humor.

From childhood the narcissist developed a false self as a result of parental expectations that he/she was perfect and superior to everyone else. Beneath the false facade the narcissist unconsciously feels worthless and fraudulent. The narcissist's perception that others are not treating him with the ultimate respect and obedience that he deserves, activates the tripwire of his narcissistic wounds and slights.

LIVING IN THE NARCISSIST'S SHADOW

The narcissist magnetizes people to him/her with his physical attractiveness, extraordinary confidence, drive, social skills, and personal appeal. In the presence of a narcissist who is very successful in the world, many of us feel uplifted, excited, more optimistic and alive. When the narcissist is at the top of his game, it is difficult to say "no" to him.

Those who are chosen to be intimates of a narcissist are picked for special reasons. Narcissists are incapable of genuine intimacy. Everyone is his possession, even a husband or wife. He is in charge and in control; he makes the rules and dictates the roles the person by his side will play. Narcissists choose individuals who are physically attractive, often younger than themselves. They are drawn to partners who are malleable, who can be modelled and worked with like pieces of clay. The narcissist's partner lacks a strong sense of self. Beneath their lovely exterior those who are destined to reside in the narcissist's shadow are emotionally dependent and suffer from deep feelings of inadequacy and worthlessness. They are like frightened children. Even if they throw tantrums and tirades at times, they return to their psychological fusion with the narcissist. Hidden inside these partners are feelings of helplessness and fury. They have struck a losing bargain. In exchange for their loyalty, they have thrown their genuine selves aside. Often their need for financial security and a luxurious lifestyles outweighs the healthy drive toward individuation, a sense of entitlement and creativity.

The childhood background of narcissistic partners has several roots. Many of these individuals are raised by parents who were neglectful, cold and indifferent. These parents never respected or loved their child as a unique individual. This child never received loving attention from the parent(s). He was dismissed with cruel messages: "Go away, I'm too busy" or "Leave me alone; I have more important things to do" or "I'm overwhelmed; I can't take care of myself, let alone you." To survive, this child learned to be compliant and became emotionally frozen.

Spouses and partners who live in the shadows of the narcissist are psychologically trapped in the survival patterns of childhood. Extricating oneself is a tall order. Many partners decide either consciously or unconsciously that it is better to play pretend at life and enjoy the fruits of the narcissist's success and savor their role as consort than to break the fusion and be left adrift and alone without internal or external resources.

SEPARATING FROM A NARCISSISTIC HUSBAND - ONE EFFECTIVE WAY TO EMPOWER YOURSELF

Need some help on separating from a narcissistic husband? Living with a narcissistic husband is really depressing and most of the time you're not given the chance to be happy with your life. This becomes really frustrating if you cannot leave him mainly because you're financially dependent with him. Your life can be a constant struggle especially if you don't know the right actions to take.

A narcissist is very deceptive because you're not going to quickly notice the warning signs. It is only after you've established the love and the trust that he will show you his true colors. You have to remember that no matter what, you have total control of your life. Healing takes time but you can recover your soul and get your life back quickly if you know where to start the healing process.

I had a friend who's in the process of separating from a narcissistic husband. She's been emotionally abused for over 20 years and later abandoned by her abusive husband to live with another woman. If you're in her situation how would you behave? What actions would you take to manipulate a narcissist?

First thing to remember is do not harbor thoughts of revenge. Why? Because your narcissistic husband will only turn against you and will only show you more cruelty. If he finds out that you no longer love him then you'll quickly have no greater importance to him and he'll simply move on and find another victim.

Instead, try to come out of this situation as winner. How? By simply letting your narcissistic husband believe that you're still head over heels in love with him.

For instance, you can send him messages telling him all your deep feelings even though he's been cruel to you.

A narcissist feels great when they know that you're lost and miserable. This will give them the validation that they're really a more powerful person. If you make your narcissistic husband believe that he's in control then you can pull his strings and make him do whatever you want.

Separating from a narcissistic husband is the best thing that you can do right now. The techniques that I've shared above is tough but it will only increase your self-confidence knowing that you're really in control of everything.

THE ESCALATING SHAMELESSNESS OF THE NARCISSIST

Shame is a primary painful feeling and bodily sensation of not being good enough, falling short, experiencing humiliation. Most of us carry some shame with us. Shame is a basic emotion that begins early in life. Some children are continuously shamed by their parent(s). The child who is frequently shamed and humiliated, feels helpless and worthless inside. He wants to disappear into the woodwork and hide from everyone. When we see a child who has been severely shamed, his eyes are cast downward. He is unable to meet our gaze. He feels so small, he wishes he didn't exist. Feelings of shame block positive human experiences like joy, humor and hopefulness. Extreme shame can keep an individual from developing close relationships with others and from enjoying life itself.

The narcissist has the opposite problem. He or she is shameless. There is nothing that disrupts the narcissist's persistent bold moves to get and have what he wants. The narcissist sees no red or amber lights ahead to make him stop or slow down. He moves at full speed toward his goal. Whether it is a lucrative business arrangement or a prospective romantic partner or spouse, the narcissist lunges ahead with extreme self entitlement, feelings of superiority and an iron will that cannot be deterred. Besides his shamelessness, the narcissist never developed much of a conscience. He will usually tow the line legally because getting caught is not an option. He cares deeply about his polished image so he is motivated to remain publicly discreet about his unscrupulous dealings.

Narcissists become particularly shameless during a divorce. They accuse the other spouse of neglecting the children when the reverse is true. They hide their assets long before the formal divorce proceedings begin. They lie about their net worth so they don't have to part with alimony or child support. Some narcissists, both male and female, abandon their families all together and start new lives with more attractive, adoring and compliant partners. Leaving the previous spouse and children in a state of financial and psychological chaos is of no consequence to them. Many narcissists repeat these egregious patterns of behavior throughout their lives without shame or regret.

Narcissists often escalate their brazen behaviors. After all, the high functioning narcissist is treated with extreme adulation and praise. He is encircled by a loyal group of admirers who provide him with a continuous cascade of compliments and special treatment. As they glide through life, many narcissists become more heartless as they grab for more. They are never satisfied with what they have. The hunger begins anew and they reach for a higher mountain of material largess and self aggrandisement. As their outrageous cruelties multiply, narcissists become even more shameless. Their raw hubris and feelings of godlike power cannot be overstated.

LIVING WITH A NARCISSISTIC LAWYER

Although it sounds like a bad lawyer joke, believe me it is no picnic living with a narcissistic attorney, especially if he is a litigator. Some of the qualities of an aggressive litigator are indicative of narcissism: arrogance, aggressiveness, self-entitlement, and grandiosity, just to name a few.

Let's be clear: having a big ego is not bad per se and in fact is essential for success in the court room. It is when one crosses over the line from healthy self esteem and confidence to high level toxic narcissism that anyone living with such a person suffers greatly. The biggest single difference that distinguishes the high-level narcissist is his total inability to empathize, which results in cruel behavior. Such behavior is ironically more common in the home than in the work place, in this instance, the court room, because the narcissist must put on an act in court, feigning great compassion.

To add insult to injury, a person who is both a high-level narcissist and a lawyer brings his litigation skills into the home in the form of "cross examination" and argumentative techniques even when he is dead wrong on the merits.

A major characteristic of a narcissistic attorney (and any narcissist for that matter) is the need to project an image of perfection. The more public the forum (such as the court room) the more the narcissist hides behind his mask of perfection. As the venue becomes smaller, the mask isn't really dropped---after all they are in fact "perfect" in their minds. However, because of their position of power in smaller groups, their need to be on their "best behavior" diminishes. This can be seen, for example, in situations such as the humiliation of an employee in front of others at office meetings. The home is the most private of all venues and thus, a spouse or other person living with a narcissist bears the greatest brunt of all.

Often the victim will say to a psychotherapist or other confidante, words to this effect: "Everyone thinks this guy is so wonderful but they should try living with this narcissistic jerk."

So---what to do? First and foremost, know yourself and stand up to the narcissist's frivolous and unfounded attacks. Calmly confront them with the inappropriateness of their behavior. If you are lucky you can sometimes "pop their balloon" using humor and at least get some temporary relief. This will not undo their pathology and may even trigger more rage. Stay empowered by tapping into your genuine sense of entitlement and self respect. Do not give your power away to them. Learn the art and skill of restraint. Not reacting is a powerful tool to use with a narcissist. They are expecting you to overreact so they can continue to pounce. You are not required to make an immediate response to an inappropriate demand. Quietly remove yourself from the situation. Give yourself a break from the drama of the battle. All of these strategies require tremendous discipline and practice.

Often it is best to seek quality professional help from a therapist who has a solid clinical background in dealing with narcissistic personalities and those who live with them. By forming a strong therapeutic alliance, the emotionally distressed client will benefit from being understood and treated with empathy. The client will have the opportunity to express the many hurtful feelings he has been holding inside so long. The therapist will assist the client in discovering his future options. This can take many forms. The client may benefit by using other strategies that allow him to be more psychologically independent from the narcissist. In some instances the therapist helps the client through the process of recognizing that the relationship is too toxic and must come to an end. In this case, the therapist works with the client in dealing with the sadness, rage, disappointment, and grief of severing a marriage or partnership. The therapeutic process will facilitate the client's recognition that he is a separate, unique, valuable human being, capable and entitled to both giving and receiving love.

10 THINGS YOU SHOULD KNOW ABOUT DEALING WITH A NARCISSIST

At some point, you've probably been forced to confront someone you would call a narcissist. But the term means more than just having a big ego. Actual narcissism is a real personality disorder in which people feel overly important, require admiration, and lack empathy for others. It's not that uncommon —about 6 percent of Americans show signs of the disorder. Since it can be incredibly challenging to deal with a narcissist, I have rounded up some expert wisdom to help get you through any future encounters with your own sanity intact.

1. NARCISSISTS HAVE ZERO TOLERANCE FOR SHAME.

They're so sensitive to issues of feeling inadequate, insecure, and shameful that they don't typically allow themselves to experience shame. If someone criticizes them, shows disappointment, or even asks for something they don't feel equipped to offer, "they will either shut down completely and get distant, avoidant, and pouty, or they will overcompensate and become critical or hostile," explains psychotherapist Wendy Behary, author of Disarming the Narcissist.

2. THE FRAGILE, INSECURE CORE OF A NARCISSIST HAS ROOTS IN CHILDHOOD.

Narcissism is thought to be a mixture of nature and nurture, according to the Mayo Clinic. There may be a genetic component, but the way a child is brought up has a lot to do with it. There are two main routes to creating an adult narcissist: As young children, they might have missed out on what it means to be cherished and loved unconditionally, so they don't feel comfortable in the emotional realm. This can lead to them spoiling relationships with obnoxious behavior or acting like a victim if they're being blamed. The other way is through being overly indulged: "You can have the purely spoiled, entitled narcissist who was just given the message as a child that they could have whatever they want when they wanted," Behary says. A new study released just this month of 565 children and their parents confirms the view that making kids believe they are overly special can lead to adult narcissism.

3. BURDENSOME EXPECTATIONS WERE OFTEN PLACED ON THEM AT A VERY EARLY AGE.

They might have been expected to perform at the highest level or be overly responsible for a parent or sibling. So as adults, "they're constantly trying to prove themselves by being a showoff or the center of attention," Behary says. "It's all in the name of trying to win approval through performance rather than just being."

4. NARCISSISTS ARE FUELED BY THE DESPERATE NEED TO BE SUPERIOR.

They may react with contempt to anyone who is perceived to have something they lack. "If someone else is one up, they are automatically one down," says expert Dr. Sandy Hotchkiss, a therapist and author of Why Is It Always About You: The Seven Deadly Sins of Narcissism. "It's not like I can be good and you can be good. It's, 'I'm better and you're worse.'"

5. NARCISSISTS TEND TO ENGAGE IN GRANDIOSE THINKING TO INSULATE THEMSELVES FROM THEIR INNER EMPTINESS.

"They may name-drop or have best this or that, and they want you to know it," Dr. Hotchkiss says. They indulge an inflated view of themselves that doesn't necessarily correspond to reality, so they may exaggerate their achievements and talents, and expect you to be impressed even if they're not all that.

6. A SENSE OF ENTITLEMENT LIES AT THE CORE OF NARCISSISTIC BEHAVIOR.

They feel they are deserving in situations without regard to other people. "Entitlement is a way to bypass their having to feel disappointed or vulnerable because they've asked for something and didn't get it," explains Dr. Craig Malkin, author of Rethinking Narcissism and an instructor of psychology at Harvard Medical School. When an extremely entitled narcissist also exhibits manipulative and exploitative behavior, that's the most troubling combination.

7. NARCISSISTS TEND TO IGNORE APPROPRIATE BOUNDARIES.

It may be up to you to make sure you're not being taken advantage of by enforcing boundaries that you establish. "It's a very, very important strategy," Behary says. "If someone's being overly aggressive or selfish, and you have a sturdy sense of yourself, say, 'This conversation is over, you can't talk to me like that.'" Other suggestions: Don't pick up every phone call and keep the ones you do pick up short.

8. NARCISSISTS RESPOND BEST TO EMPATHIC VALIDATION WHEN BEING CONFRONTED.

"Affirm the relationship first before you share anything that doesn't feel right," Dr. Malkin advises. "For example, if it's someone you're dating, say to them: 'I care about you a lot, so when you don't listen to what I'm saying, I feel like I'm nothing in your eyes,' instead of, 'Why don't you ever listen to me?'"

9. NARCISSISTS MAY BE MOTIVATED TO CHANGE IF THERE IS A MEANINGFUL CONSEQUENCE TO THEIR BAD BEHAVIOR.

Consider how much it would matter to them if you walked away from the relationship. "Don't necessarily threaten them," Behary says, "but lay it down as a solid prediction for what might happen if they don't take their behavior seriously — if they don't stop and become more responsible about the way they're hurting someone." It's not a matter of giving someone an ultimatum in an aggressive way, but rather calmly and rationally expressing the stakes if the person continues to behave that way. If the consequences are high enough, they might start to reevaluate their actions.

10. NARCISSISTS ARE EMOTIONALLY STUCK AT A TODDLER'S AGE.

"It helps to think of a narcissist as being emotionally 2 or 3 years old, like a tantrumming child," Dr. Hotchkiss says. Adds Behary: "They're just putting on a show. They're trying to get under your skin to evoke a reaction." As long as you're not in any danger, your own tolerance levels and non-negotiable values will help you dictate which battles to pick. But you might not want to go after every little thing. All the experts agree: Sometimes you just have to take the high road.

CONCLUSION

Someone with a narcissistic personality is very adept at getting exactly what they want out of a relationship - even if they have to bleed the other person dry. Sex, lies, and passive-aggressive manipulation are the three more powerful strategies in the narcissist's arsenal of emotional weapons and he will use each one to prove just how expert a marksman he truly is. Having a narcissistic personality disorder means constantly having to search and seek out new and better means of supply to fulfill his/her relationship agenda. Since a narcissist is unable to feel remorse, guilt, or any form of empathy, the fact that the main source of supply (i.e. the loving partner) must often be destroyed and resurrected over and over again matters not. The more the "good" partner suffers, the more alive the disordered partner feels - and around and around it goes.

Narcissism, unfortunately, has become an epidemic in today's social networking lifestyles. These predators enjoy the hunt of online dating where they can wear the mask quite a bit longer and catch the very vulnerable. Learning to recognize the signs and behaviors of the narcissistic personality can prevent the abuse from ever starting or give you the confidence to finally and permanently exit the game.

Printed in Great Britain
by Amazon